Wacky Wire C

Designed by Barbara Mc

This ornament is super fun and easy to make! Wire comes in all kinds of colors, so use whatever ones you like, in any combination.

1. Ask an adult to help you cut seven 2- to 3-foot lengths of wire.
2. Using one length of wire at a time, wind the wire around a pencil, straw, or dowel to create a spring.
3. Pull the springs apart to lengthen.
4. Remove the cap from the glass or plastic bulb.
5. Insert six springs into the bulb.
6. Put the last spring through the loop in the cap.
7. Replace the cap on the bulb.

Age range
8 and up (under 8 can do this project if using a plastic bulb)

You Will Need
20 to 24 gauge wire, poly-coated or metallic-colored, in any color
Glass or plastic bulb
Wire snips or heavy scissors
Pencil, straw, or dowel

Gift Package Ornament

Designed by Kathryn Severns

Dress up your tree with this festive ornament that can be decorated with any kind of sequin you like!

1. Pin the pattern on page 25 to the felt square; cut two (a front and a back).
2. Choose one felt piece for the front. With a pencil, draw the corner markings onto the front of the ornament. Outline these markings and the edges of the ornament with puffy fabric paint. Let dry thoroughly.
3. Glue sequins onto the front of the ornament. Let dry.
4. Fold the 1/8" wide ribbon in half. Glue the front and back ornament pieces together while inserting the ribbon ends between the felt layers (the ribbon makes the hanger). Let dry.
5. Make a bow with the 5/16" ribbon. Glue the bow to the front top of the ornament. Let dry.

Age range
8 and up

You Will Need
Felt square, blue
Snowflakes or any Christmas motif sequins
Puffy fabric paint, black
9" of 1/8" wide ribbon, silver
9" of 5/16" wide ribbon, silver
Glue
Scissors
Straight pins
Pencil

Cool Color-blend Pin

Designed by Barbara McGuire

This pin would make a wonderful gift for your mom, grandma, or teacher!

Age range
5 and up (young children require direct supervision)

You Will Need
Creative Paper Clay
Acrylic brayer
Plastic needlework canvas
Butter knife
Assorted buttons with textured design
Cray-Pas oil pastels and a cotton swab
Manicure sponge or sanding block
Pin backs with adhesive strip

Idea!
If you want to make an ornament instead of a pin, you can poke a hole in the top of the tree with a small straw while the clay is wet. Color both sides of the ornament and tie a ribbon through the hole to hang.

1. Using the acrylic brayer, roll the Creative Paper Clay out to a 1/8" to 1/4" sheet on the plastic needlework canvas, wide enough to fit the pattern and about 8" long. This should make four pins.

2. Place the pattern on page 25 on the clay and cut the trees along the pattern lines with the butter knife. **Note:** You can turn the pattern upside down to fit all of the trees on the sheet of clay. Take away any excess clay.

3. Press a button down the center of each tree, in a straight line. The imprint will remain in the clay.

4. Allow the pieces to completely dry (about 24 hours). **Note:** Do not put the plastic canvas in the oven to speed drying!

5. Remove the dry trees from the plastic canvas and sand the edges with the manicure sponge or sanding block. You can also sand the top to make it nice and smooth, but do not sand out the button design!

6. Using Cray-Pas, color the trees and blend the colors with your finger or the cotton swab. Lightly go over the designs with some color, but don't color the texture (this highlights the design).

7. Turn the trees over. Peel the adhesive strips off of the pin backs and attach them to the backs of the trees as shown at right.

Sparkly Star Ornament

Designed by Barbara McGuire

With sparkly embossing powder that looks like glitter, this shimmery polymer clay ornament will look pretty on your Christmas tree.

1. On card stock, condition and roll out a sheet of clay with the acrylic brayer that is approximately 1/8" thick.

2. Wind the purple wire around the straw. Because the wire is plastic coated, you may have trouble slipping it off of the straw. If this is the case, unwind the coil in the opposite direction to loosen it. Ask an adult to help you clip the ends with the wire snips or heavy scissors.

3. Pull the wire apart so it is long enough to fit around the outside of the cookie cutter. Pulling it apart will also help hold the wire in place when it is placed on the clay.

4. Use the cookie cutter as a guide to shape the wire into a star. Bend and pinch the corners and the tips so they stay in place. Have an adult help you clip any excess wire.

5. Position the wire on top of the sheet of clay, still keeping the wire in the star shape. Press it into the clay.

6. Trim around the star with the butter knife. Take away any excess clay.

7. With the straw, poke a hole in the top of one star point for the hanger hole.

8. Sprinkle glitter embossing powder on the star (it will heat set in the oven).

9. Keeping the star on the card stock, ask an adult to help you bake the star as the manufacturer directs. The wire will withstand low oven temperatures.

10. When the piece is cool, tie a 1-foot long piece of yellow wire through the hole at the top. Coil the ends with the small straw.

Age Range

8 and up (baking should be done by an adult, or, for older children, with adult supervision)

You Will Need

Sculpey polymer clay, Violet #5515
Star cookie cutter
Acrylic brayer
24 gauge plastic-coated Fun Wire™, yellow and purple, from AMACO
Small straw
Wire snips or heavy scissors
Oven
Sparkle embossing powder, silver
Butter knife
Card stock

Polymer Clay Basics

To condition clay: Before you use polymer clay, it is important to condition it (to make it softer and easier to work with). Use your hands and the acrylic brayer to make it soft and to roll it out.

Baking clay: You need to bake polymer clay to make it hard. Most often, polymer clay should be baked in an oven at 265° for 20 to 30 minutes, but make sure you read the clay package's directions for more specific instructions.

Gingerbread People Card Set

Designed by Gail Green

Do you like gingerbread people? While you can't eat these cuties, they are sure delightful on this matching card, envelope, and gift tag.

Age range

7 and up (under 7 can do this project with direct supervision)

You Will Need

- 3" x 4" piece of craft foam, any color
- 2-1/2" x 3" wood block
- Double-sided pressure-sensitive adhesive sheet and tape roll
- Dye inkpads in tan, rust, and/or brown
- Small size buttons, beads, wiggle eyes, and faux gems
- Baby rickrack, ribbon, and other assorted trims
- Scrap paper
- Scraps of decorative patterned papers and/or fabric in colors of your choice
- 5" x 7" note card, matching envelope, and gift tag
- Scissors
- Bamboo skewer
- Glue
- Pencil

Tips

- To clean your stamp, blot it clean with wet paper towels or a rag.
- Clean your stamp each time you change to a different ink color.
- Before stamping your project, practice on scrap paper.

1. To create the stamp, attach a piece of the adhesive sheet to one side of the craft foam. Trace the gingerbread pattern on page 25 onto the scrap paper. Cut out the shape and place it on the foam (the side without adhesive). Using the bamboo skewer, trace around the shape directly onto the foam. Carefully cut the shape out. Peel off the adhesive's protective paper and press the foam shape onto the wood block.

2. Apply ink to the stamp by pressing the inkpad directly onto the image until the entire foam surface is covered. Use one color or, if desired, use a combination of two or three shades to create a blended look. Practice stamping the image on scrap paper until you like the effect and to see how often you will need to reapply ink to the stamp.

3. Stamp a row of three gingerbread people on the note card and one on the envelope and gift tag. Let dry completely.

4. Decorate the gingerbread people, using the photo as a guide. Cut out one or more decorative fabric or paper jackets, following the guidelines on the pattern, and attach to the people with short strips of pressure-sensitive tape. Apply a strip of tape along the top and bottom edges of the card to attach rows of ribbon or paper. Also, apply a strip of tape along the envelope flap edges and on the bottom of the envelope front; attach a piece of ribbon or paper.

5. Use glue to attach the small buttons, eyes, rickrack, and ribbon bows to the gingerbread people. You can also cut out small hearts and decorate the envelope, as shown. Let the glue dry completely.

Interlocking Tree Card

Designed by Kathryn Severns

Today, lots of people make Christmas cards on their computers, but here is a cool card you can make and decorate with markers, sequins, colored pencils, yarn... the possibilities are endless!

Age range

7 and up

You Will Need

8-1/2" x 11" piece of card stock
4-3/8" x 5-3/4" envelope
Markers, sequins, and other decorations
Pencil
Ruler
Scissors
Butter knife
Optional: glue

1. Trace the pattern on page 25 onto the card stock (make sure you enlarge the pattern as directed). Cut out.

2. Place the ruler on each fold line and, using the dull side of the butter knife, score along the line.

3. Fold the side sections toward the center.

4. On the right side of the card, cut halfway down the tree length, starting at the top of the tree. On the left side, cut halfway up the tree length, starting at the bottom of the tree.

5. Carefully interlock the tree sections by inserting the left bottom slit into the right top slit, as shown.

6. Decorate the card as desired. Glue on any decorations that are not drawn.

7. Even though it is not shown, you can also decorate an envelope to match the card.

What Does it Mean?

Have you ever heard the word "score" before? No; not like the score in sports or games! Here, "score" means to run an object, like a butter knife, along a line on paper to make it easier to bend and fold.

PolyShrink Gift Tags

Designed by Kit Zimmerman for Lucky Squirrel

These fun PolyShrink gift tags can be used for about anything, including ornaments. Because the plastic changes size when it is baked, it is great to have a template as a record of the size of the original you started with (see pages 26 and 27 for templates). If the piece turns out just right after baking, it's easy to make more using your template.

Age range
6 and up (baking should be done by an adult, or, for older children, with adult supervision)

General Instructions for PolyShrink

1. Sand with 320 to 400 grit sandpaper in a crosshatch pattern.
2. Apply design and background color.
3. Cut out your design with regular or decorative-edge scissors.
4. Punch holes with a paper punch. Remember, the holes will shrink, too!
5. Bake on medium-weight cardboard or a Teflon sheet. Avoid baking on bare metal! Bake in a regular or toaster oven at 300° to 350° for approximately 2 minutes, or heat with an embossing heat tool.
6. After shrinking, your design will be about 45 percent of its original size and about 1/16" thick. Most pigments become permanent after shrinking.

EASY ORNAMENT

1. Sand both sides of a half sheet of Clear PolyShrink.

2. Trace the pattern on page 26 onto the PolyShrink. Cut out.

3. Use a red colored pencil to color the back of the ornament.

4. Ask an adult to draw the gold ornament hanger and write the message with a metallic marker on the front of the ornament.

5. Have an adult bake the ornament following the manufacturer's instructions.

6. Tie a bow with a ribbon, through the ornament hanger.

PRETTY SNOWFLAKE

1. Sand both sides of a half sheet of Clear PolyShrink.

2. Trace the pattern on page 26 onto the PolyShrink. Cut out.

3. Ask an adult to write a message on the front of the snowflake with a paint marker.

4. Using Colorbox Crafter's heat-setting ink and a snowflake rubber stamp, stamp images on the back of the PolyShrink. (**Note:** The rubber stamped used is from Magenta.)

5. Punch a hole in the snowflake, as shown on the pattern.

6. Have an adult bake the snowflake following the manufacturer's instructions.

7. Tie a few pieces of thin ribbon through the hole.

BRIGHT LIGHTS

1. Sand both sides of a sheet of Clear PolyShrink.

2. Trace the patterns on page 26 onto the PolyShrink. Cut out.

3. Use colored pencils to color the backs of the bulbs.

4. Use a green colored pencil for the socket, on the front and back.

5. Write the message using a fine-tip black marker on the front of the lights.

6. Punch a hole in the pieces, as shown on the patterns.

7. Have an adult bake the lights and socket following the manufacturer's instructions.

8. String the lights and socket together with ribbon.

STIPPLED TREE

1. Sand both sides of a sheet of Translucent PolyShrink.

2. Trace the patterns on page 27 onto the PolyShrink. Cut out.

3. Use chalk pastels on the front of the pieces and rub them in with your fingertips.

4. Using a paintbrush, stipple Colorbox Crafter's heat-setting ink in similar colors over the background colors.

Continued on the next page.

YOU WILL NEED FOR EACH PIECE

Note that each project uses slightly different supplies

PolyShrink™, Clear and Translucent

320 to 400 grit sandpaper

Scissors, regular or decorative-edge

Hole punch

Ribbon or string

Colored pencils, in assorted colors

Metallic and paint markers, in assorted colors (**Note:** For adults only to use in a well-ventilated area!)

Sharpie® marker, black

Medium-weight cardboard or Teflon sheet

Rubber stamps, Colorbox Crafter's® heat-setting inkpads, and sealer

Oven, toaster oven, or embossing tool

Chalk pastels

2 jump rings and pliers

Paintbrush

Pencil

BAKING TIPS

- Expect PolyShrink to curl and move during baking.
- Occasionally a piece may stick to itself as it shrinks. To separate, allow the piece to cool and pull gently. You'll hear a tiny "snap" as the joint comes apart. You can now reheat the piece and finish shrinking.
- Baked PolyShrink is very pliable while it is hot. It can be smoothed flat using cardboard or shaped over a variety of objects.

TIP

- Spraying the finished Snowflake with sealer will restore the clarity and make the stamped design easier to see.
- If you spray the Lights with sealer, it will make the colors brighter.

WHAT DOES IT MEAN?

The word "stipple" means to apply ink or paint to a surface with small, light touches. This creates a cool "shadow" effect.

To find out more about PolyShrink™, contact:
Lucky Squirrel
P.O. Box 606
Belen, NM 87002
800-462-4912
www.luckysquirrel.com

5. Ask an adult to write a message on the front of the tree base with a paint marker.

6. Punch a hole in the top and bottom of the star, top and bottom of the tree, and the top of the tree holder, as shown on the patterns.

7. Have an adult bake the tree, base, and star following the manufacturer's instructions.

8. Tie a thin ribbon through the top of the star. Ask an adult to help you connect the pieces as shown with the jump rings and pliers.

Funky Foil Gift Tags

Designed by Kathryn Severns

These neat stars can be used as gift tags, ornaments, window decorations... just use your imagination!

Age range
5 and up

You Will Need
Paragona ArtEmboss Colored Foils, gold and silver
Bamboo skewer or toothpick
Scissors
Tape
Optional: hole punch and ribbon, any color

1. Place the pattern on page 27 on the foil and trace with the bamboo skewer or toothpick. Cut out.

2. Using the bamboo skewer or toothpick, write the recipients' name and any desired designs, like trees, starts, hearts, or squiggles, on the foil star.

3. You can attach the star with tape to a gift or punch a hole in the top, string ribbon through the hole, and tie it to the gift.

Polar Bear and Reindeer Gift Bags

Designed by Mary Ayres

Decorating plain gift bags is fun and easy. The polar bear and reindeer are made with decorative stencils from Fiskars, which make it easy to get the exact shapes you need!

Age range
8 and up

You Will Need

6" x 11" paper bags, blue and green, from Bemiss-Jason

Cardstock or construction paper, white, red, purple, light blue, bright blue, black, tan, medium brown

Translucent vellum paper, white

Basic shapes decorative stencil, Theme 1, from Fiskars

9/16" circle punch shape from Fiskars

1/4" circle hand punch from Fiskars

Hippo Kidzors paper edgers from Fiskars

Snowflakes 3-in-1 corner punch from Fiskars

Zig Memory System 2 Way Glue pen from EK Success

Zig Memory System fine-tip permanent marker, black, from EK Success

Scissors

Pencil

Ruler

1. Trim the top edges of the bags using the Kidzors. Cut two 4-1/2" x 8-1/2" rectangles from light blue paper. Punch a snowflake shape from each of the rectangle corners. Glue a rectangle to the center front of each bag.

2. Cut two 3-1/2" x 6-1/2" rectangles from purple paper using the Kidzors. Glue a purple rectangle to the center of each light blue rectangle.

3. To make snowflakes, draw four 2-1/8" circles on vellum paper and cut out with scissors. Fold the circles in half, then in half again, and once more. Cut out small shapes from the edges of the folded circles. Cut each circle differently, because each snowflake should be unique! Unfold the snowflakes. Glue two snowflakes to each bag front, around the animal heads, after you have completed the instructions on the next page.

Continued on the next page.

Polar Bear

To make the bear, use the stencil template to draw three 2-1/8" circles for the muzzle and ears and one 4" oval for the head, all from white paper. Cut out the shapes with scissors. Punch a 9/16" circle from bright blue paper for the nose. Punch two 1/4" circles from black paper for the eyes. Punch one 1/4" circle from white paper for the nose dot. Draw the muzzle details and a wiggly line around each of the bear pieces (except eyes and nose dot) close to the edges with the black marker. Following the pattern on page 27, glue the ears to the back of the head. Glue the muzzle and eyes to the front of the head. Glue the nose to the muzzle. Glue the nose dot to the nose. Glue the assembled bear head to the center front of the blue bag at an angle.

Reindeer

To make the reindeer, use the stencil template to draw one 2-1/8" circle for the ears and one 4" oval for the head, all from brown paper, and one 4" heart for the antlers from tan paper. Cut out the shapes with scissors, cutting the ear circle in half. Punch a 9/16" circle from red paper for the nose. Punch two 1/4" circles from black paper for the eyes. Punch one 1/4" circle from white paper for the nose dot. Draw the mouth and antler details and a wiggly line around each of the reindeer pieces (except the eyes and nose dot) close to the edges with the black marker. Following the pattern on page 28, glue the ears and antlers to the back of the head. Glue the nose and eyes to the front of the head. Glue the nose dot to the nose. Glue the assembled reindeer head to the center front of the green bag at an angle.

Snowman Jar Surround

Designed by Barbara Matthiessen

This creative container is made from an old jar and surrounded by cute craft foam snowmen. While it can be used as a centerpiece, it would also make a great gift jar filled with candy or cookies.

1. Trace four snowman patterns on page 28 onto the white foam with a marker. You can trace around the center part of your jar lid for the center pattern, or use the pattern on page 28 for the lid. Trace the lid pattern onto the white foam. Trace eight mittens onto the blue foam. Cut out all pieces just inside of the traced lines. To get smoother lines, turn the scissors as you work.

2. Shade all foam pieces with the blue pen and stiff bristled brush. To shade the mittens, draw a blue line along the edges then brush with the stiff-bristled brush toward the center to achieve a shaded look. (**Note:** In order to have four "left" mittens and four "right" mittens, make sure to turn half of the mittens over before shading them.) Run the bristles across the pen then onto the foam to softly shade all snowman edges. Wash the brush in soapy water and dry. Run the bristles over the pink pen then swirl them onto the snowman faces for cheeks in areas indicated by dashed lines on the pattern.

3. Transfer the details onto each snowman as shown on the patterns by using graphite paper and a pencil.

4. Draw the noses in with yellow and red pens to make orange. Use the white marker to draw snowflake marks on the mittens.

5. Use the black marker to draw in eyes, mouths, and buttons, to outline the noses, and to draw wiggly lines around the snowman outlines. Draw wiggly outlines and cuff lines on all mittens with the black marker.

6. Highlight the eyes and cheeks with white paint dots applied with a toothpick.

7. Glue the mitten cuffs to the sides of each snowman. Glue the round face to the lid.

8. Tear five 1" wide strips of plaid fabric for the scarves. Apply glue to the outside of the jar lid. Tie a fabric strip around the jar lid and knot. Glue a button to the knot. Tie fabric strips around each snowman's neck with a knot.

9. Stitch the snowmen together with perle cotton and embroidery needle just under the mittens where marked on the pattern. Allow extra perle cotton to adjust the fit on the jar if needed. Tie the perle cotton ends into a bow between each snowman.

10. Slide the joined snowmen over the jar and adjust the bows at the sides if needed to fit.

AGE RANGE

8 and up (under 8 can do this project with direct adult supervision)

YOU WILL NEED

1 sheet Westrim® craft foam, white
1/4 sheet Westrim® craft foam, blue
Acrylic paint, white
Zig Writers® pigment ink pens, pink, blue, yellow, red
Zig Millennium™ 08 marker, black
Zig Opaque marker, white
Beacon's Kid's Choice glue
Perle cotton, white
Scraps of fabric, plaid
3/4" button
Scissors
Stiff bristled paintbrush, such as a small stencil brush or fabric painting brush
Graphite paper
Pencil
Embroidery needle
Toothpick

Rope-wrapped Snowman

Designed by Kathleen George, made with STYROFOAM brand foam

This cute snowman will look right at home on a tabletop or fireplace mantel!

Age range
10 and up

You Will Need
STYROFOAM* brand foam, 3", 4", and 5" balls
Approx. 25 yards soft 1/4" rope
18" x 2" piece of felt, cranberry
Two 9 mm eyes
1" x 3/16" dowel
Acrylic paint, orange
Crochet thread, black
Felt, pink
Optional: buttons
Hat with 4-1/2" brim
Serrated knife
Hot glue gun and glue stick
White craft glue
Optional: straight pins
Masking tape
Utility knife
Scissors
Paintbrush
*Trademark of The Dow Chemical Company

For more information about STYROFOAM brand foam, see the following website: www.styrofoam-crafts.com

1. Ask an adult to help you slice a bit off the top and bottom of the 5" and 4" balls with the serrated knife. Slice a bit off the bottom of the 3" ball.

2. Have an adult help you glue the balls together into a snowman form with hot glue.

3. Beginning at the bottom, glue the rope onto the snowman using white craft glue. Keep wrapping and gluing until you reach the top. Pin with straight pins to secure, if needed.

4. Make arms by tying six pieces of 11" rope together; tie a knot 1" from one end. Place a bit of glue on the knot to secure. Repeat for the other arm.

5. Braid the rope arms to the end and wrap with tape.

6. Make holes in the sides of the snowman with the point of a pair of scissors. Place craft glue in the holes and push the taped end of the arms into the holes.

7. Ask an adult to help you point a piece of dowel with a utility knife. Paint orange.

8. Cut little circles of pink felt for the cheeks and a short length of crochet thread for a mouth.

9. Glue on beads for the eyes. Push the orange dowel nose into the face. Secure with a dot of glue.

10. Glue on the cheeks and mouth.

11. Glue on buttons, if desired.

12. Fringe the ends of the cranberry felt. Tie the scarf around the snowman's neck.

13. Put the hat on the snowman's head.

14. Glue the left rope hand onto the hat to make the snowman tip his hat, if desired.

Funnel Tree

Designed by Cindy Groom-Harry® and CMC Staff

Making and decorating this tree is so much fun you may want to make one to keep and one to give as a gift!

1. **Optional:** Ask an adult to cut off the handles from the plastic funnels. With an adult's help, spray the inside and out with Primer in a well-ventilated area and let dry. Now, spray with Holiday Green and let dry.

2. Referring to the photo, with an old paintbrush or craft stick, place snow around the base of each funnel. Let dry overnight.

3. Use the hand drill and bit to carefully drill a hole in the top of each Woodsies shape, except nine of the medium Circles.

4. **Optional:** For ease in painting Woodsies, use a stapler to attach Con-Tact paper, sticky-side-up, to cardboard. Remove the release paper and position all Woodsies onto the adhesive side of Con-Tact paper with approximately 1/4" between each piece and 1" between each color. Referring to the photo, paint both sides of the Woodsies pieces as follows and let dry:
    Gingerbread Men: Terra Cotta, detail with Titanium White and Marker.
    Light Bulbs: Lemon Yellow (2), True Blue (2), Shimmering Silver, Titanium highlight, and Marker.
    Stockings: Primary Red, Titanium White, Holly Green, and Marker.
    Candy Canes: Primary Red and Titanium White.
    Round Candies: Primary Red and Titanium White.
    Angel: Titanium White, Hi-Lite Flesh, Terra Cotta (hair), details with Shimmering Silver, Primary Red, and Marker.

5. Ask an adult to help you stack and glue three Circles together and six Circles together as spacers. Glue three Circles to the top inside of the medium funnel. Also, glue the six Circles to the top inside of the small funnel. Glue the medium funnel to the top of the large funnel and the small funnel to the top of the medium funnel.

Age Range
9 and up

You Will Need

3 plastic funnels: small, medium, and large

Forster Woodsies™ (Forster® Basic Woodsies™ I and Christmas Woodsies™ I and II; **Note:** If covering the entire tree, double the number of pieces, except for Circles, for which you only add two more)
    4 medium Gingerbread Men
    1 large Angel
    3 medium Candy Canes
    5 medium Light Bulbs
    3 medium Stockings
    11 medium (3/4") Circles

Design Master® COLORTOOL® Spray Paint, Holiday Green and Primer

DecoArt™ Americana® Acrylic Paint: Primary Red, True Blue, Titanium White, Lemon Yellow, Hi-Lite Flesh, Holly Green, Terra Cotta, Dazzling Metallics® Shimmering Silver

Deco Art™ Patio Paint Outdoor Snow

5 feet of 24 gauge Fun Wire, Clear/Silver, from AMACO

Optional: 10" x 12" piece of Con-Tact® paper, 10" x 12" piece of lightweight cardboard, stapler

Zig® Millennium™ marker, black, from EK Success

Craft snips and needle nose pliers

White Nylon Series 795-F, Size 3 and 00 Round Paintbrushes, from Loew-Cornell®

Old paintbrush or craft stick

Small hand drill and 1/4" drill bit

Adhesive Technologies Professional I Glue Gun and Crafty® Magic Melt® Glue Sticks

Continued on the next page.

13

6. Have an adult help you cut a 4-foot length of silver wire with craft snips. Turn one end of wire with needle nose pliers and make a small loop. String the ornaments on the wire, leaving approximately 2" to 2-1/2" between the ornaments and kinking the wire as you go. Turn the end of the wire to make a tiny loop behind the last ornament.

7. Apply glue to one end of wire and place in the hole at the top of the tree. Refer to the photo and arrange the garland around tree. Spot glue to the tree to help keep the garland in place when you like how the tree looks.

8. To make the halo, cut a 3" length of silver wire with an adult's help, make a loop around your finger, and twist the end around the base. Have an adult hot glue to the back of the angel. Glue the angel to the top of the tree.

Santa Snow Globe

Designed by Kathryn Severns

Using a glass jar and some cute Christmas figures, you can make a gift that friends and relatives will love.

Age range
10 and up

You Will Need

Empty round glass jar and lid
Spray paint, gold
Sandpaper
STYROFOAM brand foam, ball approximately equal in diameter to the jar lid
Plastic Santa and tree figurines
Glycerin
Frosted glitter
Silicone sealant
Water
Strand of faux pearls
Clear paddlewheel beads
Clear faceted beads
Glue
Scissors
Serrated knife
Tablespoon

1. Wash and dry the glass jar.

2. Lightly sand the lid. With an adult's help, spray the outside with gold spray paint in a well ventilated area, according to the manufacturer's directions. Let dry.

3. Ask an adult to help you cut a dome-shaped section of the ball to fit inside of the lid. Trim the edge of the cut piece with scissors to allow enough space around the edges to reseal the jar.

4. Glue the piece cut in Step 3 inside of the lid using silicone sealant, following the manufacturer's directions. Let dry.

5. Glue the figurines on top of the foam with silicone sealant, placing the figures toward the center and making sure the jar will fit over them. Let dry. (**Note:** Use only plastic figures; paper will disintegrate over time in water.)

6. Fill the jar with water and add 1 to 2 tablespoons of glycerin. Mix.

7. Add a little glitter to the water. **Note:** Some glitter will float to the surface; remove the floating glitter. Repeat the process until the desired amount of glitter is in the water.

8. Squeeze a ring of silicone sealant between the Styrofoam and side of the lid. Let dry.

9. Over a sink, carefully replace the lid on jar, placing the figurines inside of the jar and allowing excess water and air to escape.

10. Twist the lid shut and let dry.

11. Glue the strand of pearls around the lid.

12. Decorate the jar's top by gluing on paddlewheel and faceted beads.

Elf Countdown

Designed by Cindy Groom-Harry® and CMC Staff

Who says a Christmas countdown calendar has to hang on a wall? The CMC staff created a great way to count down to the big day— and keep things smelling nice!

1. Ask an adult to help you cut a 1" diameter slice off the bottom of the foam ball using the serrated knife. Lightly sand the seam of the foam ball to make it smooth. Paint the ball head with two coats of Flesh Tone and let dry. Ask an adult to use a glue gun to glue the cut edge of the ball to the top of the Renuzit topper.

2. Sand the base of the Renuzit to a rough surface. Paint with two coats of Kelly Green and let dry. Cut the coat from Pirate Green felt according to the pattern on page 29. Wrap and glue the coat around the topper, overlapping edges at center back.

3. Cut a 3" x 4" rectangle from Pirate Green felt. Roll and glue into a cylinder with 4" edges slightly overlapping. For the cuff, cut a 3/4" x 3" piece of White plush felt and glue around the lower edge of the sleeve. For the shoulder, crimp the narrow end of the sleeve, tuck under the ends, and glue to the top of the coat as shown on the following page. Repeat to make and attach the other sleeve. Ask an adult to use craft snips to cut two 4" lengths of chenille stems. Insert and glue the stems to the shoulder end of the sleeves. Stuff the sleeves slightly with fiberfill.

Age range
10 and up

You Will Need

The Dial Corporation Renuzit® LongLast® Adjustable Air Freshener

Forster® Woodsies™ (Christmas Woodsies™ I and II)

   3 medium Oval
   2 small, 4 medium, 3 large Circles
   1 medium Triangle
   2 medium Squares
   2 large Angels
   1 large Tree
   2 small, 1 medium, 1 large Candy Cane
   1 large Cottage
   2 small, 1 medium, 1 large Stocking
   1 medium, 1 large Santa
   1 medium, 1 large Light Bulb

DecoArt™ Americana® Acrylic Paint, Kelly Green, Flesh Tone, Lavender, Tangelo Orange, Holly Green, Titanium White, Primary Red, Terra Cotta, True Blue, Baby Pink, Lemon Yellow, Ebony Black, Dazzling Metallics® Shimmering Silver

2-1/2" diameter hard pressed foam ball

Continued on the next page.

Continued on the next page.

YOU WILL NEED, CONT.

Rainbow™ Felt and Plush Felt, from Kunin:
   9" x 12" piece, Pirate Green
   1-1/2" x 2-1/2" piece, Red
   1-1/2" x 2" piece, French Vanilla
   2" x 8" piece, White Plush Felt

15mm red jingle bell

Small amount of fiberfill

12" chenille stem, green

8" x 12" piece of fabric, holiday print

12" of 1/8" wide ribbon, red satin

Two 12 mm oval wiggle eyes

Optional: 2-1/4" doll eyeglasses

Zig® Millennium™ markers, black and red

Aleene's® Original Tacky Glue

White Nylon, Series 797-F, Size 6 and 2 Flat Stain Paintbrushes and Series 801 Size 0 Liner Brush, from Loew-Cornell®

Scissors

Fine sand paper

Ruler

Paper

Pencil

Pen

Toothpick

Optional: Tape

Craft snips

Serrated knife

Adhesive Technologies Professional I Glue Gun and Crafty® Magic Melt™ Glue Sticks

---

When the original gel from the Renuzit LongLast Adjustable Air Freshener is depleted, simply replace with a new container base. If your project base is decorated, remove dried gel. From a new container, remove new, non-toxic gel. Then slip it over the post of the decorated base and reposition the decorated topper.

For FREE Renuzit Adjustable Air Freshener Craft Project sheets, send $1 (postage and handling) and a long self-addressed envelope to:
Renuzit Crafts
Cindy Groom-Harry®,
2363 - 460th St., Dept. K-Elf
Ireton, IA 51027

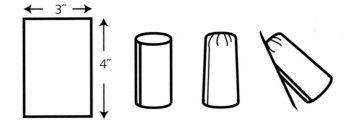

4. Cut two mittens from Red felt according to the pattern on page 29. Glue the mittens to the other ends of the chenille stems.

5. Cut two ears from French Vanilla felt according to the pattern on page 29. Position and use glue to attach the ears to the sides of the head.

6. Cut the hat from Pirate Green felt according to the pattern on page 29. Roll and glue into a cone, slightly overlapping the edges. For the hat brim, cut a 3/4" x 8" piece of White plush felt and glue around the lower edge of the hat. Position and glue the hat on the head. Glue the red jingle bell to the pointed end of the hat. Fold over the top of the hat and tack glue to the side of the hat brim.

7. Position and glue wiggle eyes to the face. Refer to the photo to lightly draw and paint the nose Baby Pink, tongue Primary Red, and mouth Ebony Black (or use a black marker). Position glasses on the face and trim or bend stems to fit. Glue the glasses to the head.

8. Cut an 8" x 12" piece of holiday print fabric. Fold in half lengthwise, with right sides together, and glue the 12" edges together using a 1/4" seam allowance. Hand-gather the bag along the 8" edge and wrap the remaining length of chenille stem close to the end, twist the ends together to secure, and trim ends. Turn the bag right side out. Fold the top edge to the inside to form a finished edge and glue to hold. Stuff the bag with a small amount of fiberfill. Using red satin ribbon, find the center of ribbon and glue to the back of the bag, approximately 2" from the top. Wrap the ribbon loosely around the bag and tie into a bow.

9. Referring to the finished photo on page 15, mix and match shapes to paint as gifts. (**Examples:** Two small stockings and a large circle will make a plate of cookies. Two small circles and an oval can be a skateboard. Cut a toothpick in half, attach one end to a medium circle for a lollipop and combine the other end with medium triangle and large oval for a sailboat.) Use the liner brush and paint or markers to add details to the shapes. Write numbers on the gifts with a black marker. Begin the countdown to Christmas by placing a "gift" in or around the Elf's bag and hand. Roll a piece of tape with sticky side out to temporarily attach gifts. Then, add one gift to the elf and his bag each day. On Christmas day, add the angel to the Elf's hand.

Angel Stocking

Designed by Chris Malone

Santa won't be able to resist stuffing this stocking with goodies!

1. Use the stocking pattern on page 30 to cut the stocking front from neon blue felt (make sure you enlarge the pattern as directed). Pin the blue front on the gold felt and cut out the stocking back 1/2" larger than the blue front on the sides and bottom. Cut even with the front at the top. Remove the pins and set the gold aside.

2. Using the patterns on page 29, trace the angel dresses and wings on the paper side of the iron-on adhesive, making two sets of wings in one direction and one in the opposite direction. Cut out about 1/8" from lines. Following the manufacturer's directions and with an adult's help, iron the adhesive to the wrong side of the fabrics (white print for wings and red print for dresses). Use the star pattern on page 29 to cut out four stars from gold felt. Cut out the appliqués on the traced lines and remove the paper backing. Place the angel pieces and stars on the stocking front, as shown in the photo, with the top of the dresses overlapping the bottom of the wings 1/4". When you like the arrangement, remove the stars and fuse the angels to the felt with an adult's help. Then, pin the stars back in place and use one strand of red Perle cotton or three strands of embroidery floss to attach each star with a running stitch close to the edge. Using gold sewing thread, sew a red button to the center of each star.

3. Center the blue stocking front on top of the stocking back, lining up the top edge, and pin to hold layers together. Using one strand of white perle cotton or three strands of floss, attach the two pieces with a blanket stitch around the edge of the stocking front, leaving it open at the top (see page 20 for blanket stitch instructions).

4. With the stocking right side up, place the zigzag pattern on page 30 on the edge of the stocking back and draw cutting lines with the air erasable or other fine-tip pen. Move the pattern to continue drawing lines. When going around a curve, move the pattern with each line. Zigzag lines do not need to be perfectly even. Cut on lines. (If you use a regular marker, cut just inside the line so marks are removed.)

Age range
9 and up

You Will Need

10" x 16" piece Rainbow® Classic Felt, neon blue and gold, from Kunin

3" x 6" fabric, white print

4" x 7" fabric, red print

1/8 yard iron-on adhesive

Perle cotton, size 5, or embroidery floss, red and white

Four 9/16" buttons, red

Three 1" wood plugs

Acrylic paints, flesh, pink, black, white

24" of 3/8" wide ribbon, wire-edged if desired, white

1 yard loopy blonde doll hair yarn

Sewing thread, gold and tan

3/4" to 1" plastic ring

Air-erasable pen or fine-line marker

Thick craft glue

Pencil

Scissors

Iron

Embroidery needle

Straight pins

Small stencil brush

Paintbrush

Paper towel and toothpick

Continued on next page.

17

5. Paint the wood plugs with flesh-colored paint. Dip the stencil brush into the pink paint and remove excess paint on a paper towel. Tap the brush to each face for cheeks. Dip the toothpick into the black paint and touch to the face for the eyes. (Re-dip for each eye so they are the same size.) Make a white highlight dot on each cheek in the same way.

6. Glue a head on each angel. Cut the ribbon into three 8" lengths and tie each in a small bow. Glue a bow under each angel's face.

7. Cut the doll hair yarn into three 12" lengths. For each angel, wrap a piece of yarn around two or three fingers held together to make a small bundle, and then slip off fingers. Thread the needle with tan thread and wrap around the center of the yarn bundle. Apply a dot of glue to the center and push down on the angel's head. Add more glue where needed.

8. Turn the stocking over. Stitch the plastic ring to the upper left corner to hang the stocking.

Cookie Recipe Garland

Designed by Kathryn Severns

You can make a gift that the cook in your family can display proudly all year long.

Age range

5 and up (with an adult helping younger children to write or type recipes)

You Will Need

6 feet of sisal rope
1/8 yard fabric, green check
1/8 yard fabric, red check
8-1/2" x 11" paper, green and red
3" x 5" index cards
Your favorite cookie recipes
Wooden spoons
Cookie cutters
Ruler
Scissors
Pen
Hole punch
Optional: computer

18

1. Cut the fabric into 5/8" wide strips. Cut the strips into 7" lengths.

2. Tie the fabric strips to the rope, alternating red and green fabric.

3. Tie cookie cutters to the rope with fabric strips at each end and then at 1-1/2-foot intervals.

4. Tie wooden spoons to the rope with fabric strips, between the cookie cutters.

5. Measure and cut red and green paper into 3-1/2" x 5-1/2" rectangles. With a pen, write recipes onto the 3" x 5" index cards.
Optional: Type the recipes using a computer.

6. Center one recipe on each red or green paper rectangle. Punch a hole in the top of both. Thread a fabric strip through the hole using green fabric for red rectangles and red fabric for green rectangles.

7. Tie the recipes onto the rope on either side of the wooden spoons, alternating red and green paper rectangles.

Santa Banner

By Chris Malone

A banner is a bright and cheerful way to announce the holiday season, and this one is a snap to make.

1. Cut a 12" x 20" rectangle from Pirate Green felt and an 8" x 13" rectangle from the Black. Use the patterns on pages 30 to 32 (enlarging some as directed) to cut four mittens and four boots from the Black; two hats and three 1-1/4" x 2" rectangles from the Red; two beards and four mustache pieces from the White; two faces and one nose from the Apricot; and three "H"s and three "O"s from the Lime colored felt. Cut two hat trims and one hat pompom from the White Plush felt. Cut one face circle from cardboard.

2. Pin the letters to the black rectangle as shown in the photo with a 1-1/2" margin at top and bottom and a 1-1/4" side margin. Attach the letters to the background with dark green

Continued on the next page.

Age range
9 and up

You Will Need

Rainbow® Classic Felt from Kunin:
  1/3 yard Pirate Green and 1/4 yard Black (each 36" wide yardage)
  9" x 12" two White, one each Lime, Red, Apricot
  3-1/2" x 9" piece White Plush

Embroidery floss, dark green, white, black

Sewing thread, red

Buttons, two 1/2", black, and one 5/8" shank, any color

15 red pompoms, 7 mm

5" square cardboard

1" x 12" x 14" wood slat

Two small sawtooth hangers

Small amount fiberfill stuffing

Thick craft glue

Scissors

Ruler

Straight pins

Embroidery needle

Hammer

Note: Use three strands of embroidery floss for all sewing unless otherwise directed.

19

floss and a running stitch. For each "O" wreath, make a bow by gathering the center of a 1-1/4" x 2" Red felt rectangle with red sewing thread. Pull tightly and knot thread. Glue to the bottom of the wreath. Glue the five red pompoms around each wreath.

3. Pin the black piece on the green rectangle right side up, with a 2" margin on each side and at the bottom and a 5" margin at the top. Attach the two pieces with green floss and blanket stitch around the black felt. Turn the banner over to the back. Apply glue to one flat side of the wood slat and press to the top of the banner. Apply glue to the other flat side of the slat, fold the slat over, and press down. Using the hammer, attach a sawtooth hanger to each end of the felt-covered slat on the back.

4. For each boot front, thread the needle with a 15" length of white floss, all six strands, and sew three "X"s down one side of boot, starting 1" down from top of boot. Knot floss and clip. With floss remaining in needle, take a small stitch at the bottom of "X"s and tie the ends in a bow. Pin the boot front and back together and sew the edges with a running stitch using white floss. Stuff lightly through the top of the boot and glue the top edges together.

5. For each mitten, pin a front and back together and sew a running stitch with the white floss along edges. Stuff lightly with fiberfill before closing. Make two mittens facing opposite directions.

6. Make mustache halves in the same way as for the mittens, using black floss. For the beard, use black floss to blanket stitch the edges of the front and back; do not stuff.

7. For the face, sew buttons to one felt circle with black floss. Glue the back of the face to one side of the cardboard and the remaining felt circle to the back. Glue the top of the beard on the face and glue the mustache halves on the top of the beard. For the nose, sew gathering stitches around the edge of the felt circle. Place the shank button in the center of the circle and pull the thread to gather the felt around the button. (Clip off the shank if it is too long.) Glue the nose above and between the mustache.

8. For the hat, pin the front and back together and sew blanket stitch around edges with black floss. Leave open at the bottom. Slip the hat over top of the head and glue in place. Glue one hat trim to the bottom of the hat on the front and back, covering the bottom edges of the hat and top of the beard. For the hat pompom, sew gathering stitches around the plush felt circle. Place a ball of fiberfill in the center of the felt on the wrong side and pull the thread to gather the felt into a ball. Glue the side with stitches to the tip of the hat.

9. Apply glue to the bottom 1-1/2" of the head on the back and press to the top center front of the banner.

10. Glue one mitten to each side at the top so Santa appears to be holding the banner. Glue the top front of the boots to the bottom back of the banner at the center so they hang down.

How to Stitch...

To blanket stitch, insert the needle below the edge of the felt to the other side so that the needle shows beyond the edge of the felt. Loop the perle cotton under the needle and pull it through with the thread below the needle.

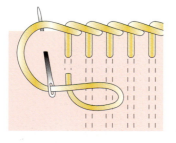

What Does It Mean?

A "shank" is the little piece (the projection) on the back of a solid button.

"Cookies For Santa" Plate And Mug

Designed by Dorris Sorensen

Your specially decorated cookie plate will make Santa's visit to your house one he can't forget!

Age range
8 and up

You Will Need

Glass plate and mug
Delta Permenamel® Surface Conditioner
Delta Permenamel® Paint Colors, Red, Candy Apple Green, Ultra White
Delta Permenamel® Gloss Glaze
Compressed sponge
Cosmetic sponges
Large paintbrush or sponge brush
Small paintbrush
Craft knife
Optional: pencil, paper, tape, round paintbrush

1. Thoroughly wash and dry the glass pieces. When they are dry, use a large paintbrush or sponge brush and apply a generous coat of Permenamel Surface Conditioner to all surfaces to be painted (the center part on the back and the rim on the front). This is a very important step, because this is what will make your paint stick to the glass and make it washable.

2. The center of the plate is painted on the back. Using a pencil eraser and Ultra White paint, make several big White dots on the back of plate. Using the wooden end of a paintbrush handle, fill in between the big dots with various size smaller dots, as shown. Allow to dry.

3. Using a piece of cosmetic sponge, sponge on two to three coats of Red over the White dots.

4. **Optional:** Write the words "Cookies for Santa" on a piece of paper. Tape this under the rim of your plate. Using a round brush, fill in the letters using Ultra White.

This plate is shown on blue to highlight the white writing.

Continued on the next page.

5. Trace the Holly Leaf pattern on page 32 onto a piece of compressed sponge. Ask an adult to help you cut the sponge. Expand the sponge in water and blot out any excess moisture.

6. Dip the leaf shape into Candy Apple Green and sponge holly leaves on the front rim of the plate.

7. Using the wooden end of the paintbrush, make a cluster of three Red dots at the base of each leaf. Let dry. Place a smaller White dot on each Red dot.

8. Using a piece of cosmetic sponge dipped in Red, carefully run it around the edge of the plate. Let dry.

9. Using a cosmetic sponge, apply a coat of Gloss Glaze to the bottom of the plate for added protection. (If you want, you can also put it over the rest of your design.)

10. Following the directions on the product bottles, allow your pieces to cure for 7 to 10 days before putting in the dishwasher, oven, or microwave.

11. Follow the instructions above to paint the mug with dots and holly leaves.

Candy Cane Coasters

Designed by Joan Green

These brightly colored coasters make the perfect gift for anyone. Just stack them up, tie a ribbon around them, and they are ready to go!

Age range
10 and up

You Will Need

1/2 sheet #7 mesh plastic canvas
#16 tapestry needle
Red Heart Kids Yarn™
   8 yards 2390 Red
   6 yards 2001 White
   10 yards 2652 Lime
   10 yards 2677 Green
   25 yards 2845 Blue
1 package Presto Felt, royal blue, from Kunin
Scissors

1. Cut four pieces of canvas, each 23 by 23 holes.

2. Follow the pattern below. The entire design is worked in Tent Stitch. First stitch one row of Lime Green all around the outer edge of the coaster. Next work the White areas of the candy canes followed by the Red stitches. Next work the holly leaves. Take one long straight stitch with the Lime Green yard to complete the holly leaves. Fill in the background with Blue.

3. Overcast the outer edge with the Green yarn, taking three stitches in each corner hole to completely cover the canvas edge.

4. Cut four pieces of felt, each 3-1/4" by 3-1/4". Peel off the paper backing and affix the felt squares to the backs of the coasters.

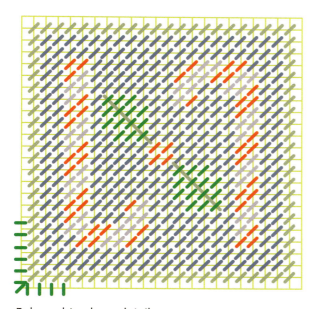

Red
White
Lime
Green
Blue

Enlarged to show detail.

How to Stitch...

These coasters are made using the Tent and Overcast stitches.

Tent Stitch

This stitch is worked over one thread. Following the diagram, bring your needle up at 1 and the rest of the odd numbers and take it down at 2 and the rest of the even numbers.

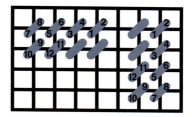

Overcast Stitch

You will be doing the Overcast stitch around the entire outer edge of each coaster. Following the diagram, bring your needle up at 1 and the rest of the odd numbers and take it down at 2 and the rest of the even numbers. At the corners, you will need to make three stitches to cover the edges.

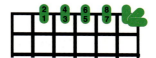

My Christmas List Scrapbook Page

Designed by Julie Stephani

Write a letter to Santa on a scrapbook page and use stickers in place of some of the words! Write out your Wish List and put it in a pocket on the page. Pick one of your favorite photos to include on the page. Wouldn't this be fun to do every year and collect all of your pages in an album?

Age range

5 and up (with an adult helping younger children to write the letter and list)

You Will Need

8-1/2" x 11" paper, white and red polka-dot
Polka-dot paper, red and green
Plain paper, red and yellow
1-1/8" sticker letters, red
Christmas stickers
Photo
Black pen
Scissors
Pencil
Photo-safe glue
Ruler

1. Use the ruler to draw a line and cut off 1/2" on the top and one side of the white paper. Center and glue the white paper on the red polka-dot paper.

2. Glue the photo on the green paper. Draw a line 1/4" from the photo edge and cut along the line. Glue the photo on the page so the top corners go off of the page. Turn the page over and cut off the corners even with the page.

3. Press sticker letters on top of the page at different angles. Press Christmas lights on the letters. Use the black pen to draw dash lines around the letters.

4. To make the pocket, cut a 3-1/2" x 5" green polka-dot rectangle. Draw a thin line of glue along the sides and bottom of rectangle, NOT THE TOP. Press onto the bottom of the page. Cut a 1-1/2" x 2-1/4" white rectangle. Glue it on red polka-dot paper. Draw a line 1/4" from the edge and cut along the line. Center and glue on the pocket. Press three stocking stickers on the white rectangle. Print your Christmas list on a 3-1/2" square of yellow paper and put it in the pocket.

5. Use the black pen to write a letter to Santa. Use stickers in place of some of the words. Be sure to print Christmas and the year somewhere on your page.

Patterns

To trace any of the patterns in this book, use a pencil and tracing paper. Some of the patterns will need to be enlarged. Ask an adult to help you use a photocopier to enlarge the pieces as directed.

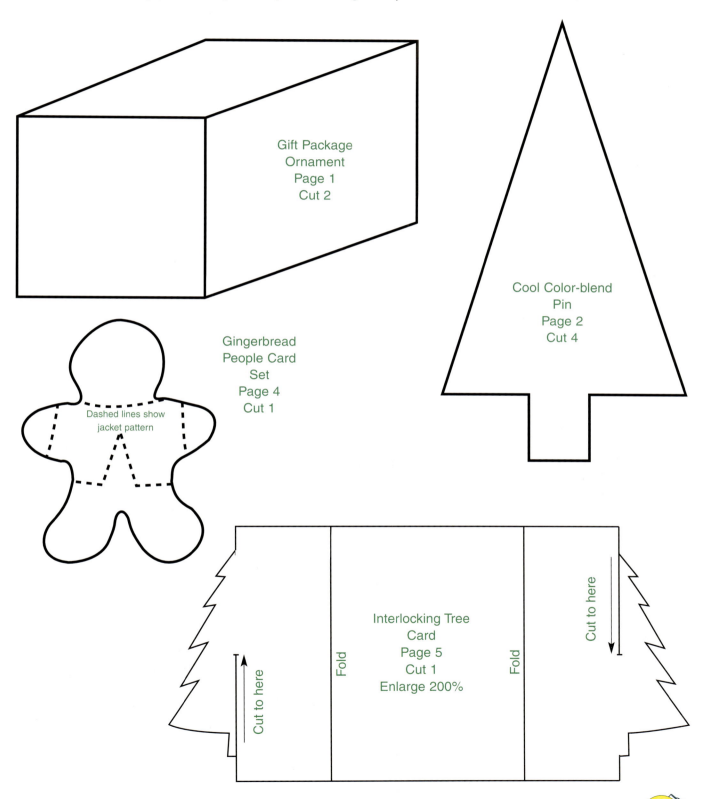

Gift Package Ornament
Page 1
Cut 2

Cool Color-blend Pin
Page 2
Cut 4

Gingerbread People Card Set
Page 4
Cut 1

Dashed lines show jacket pattern

Interlocking Tree Card
Page 5
Cut 1
Enlarge 200%

Fold

Cut to here

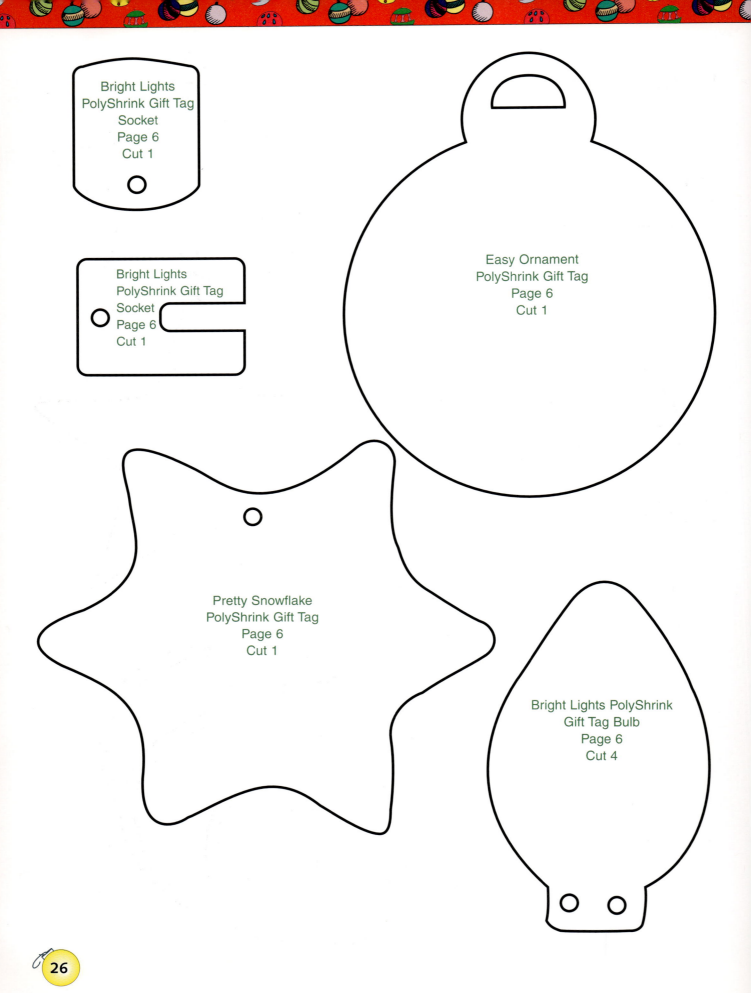

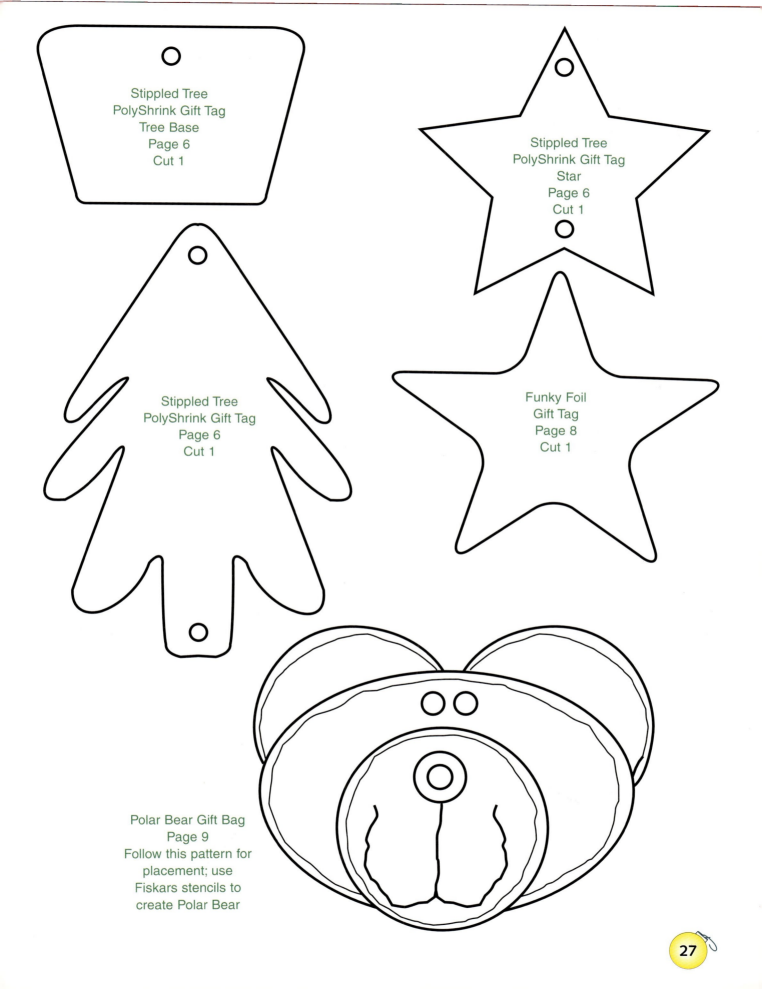

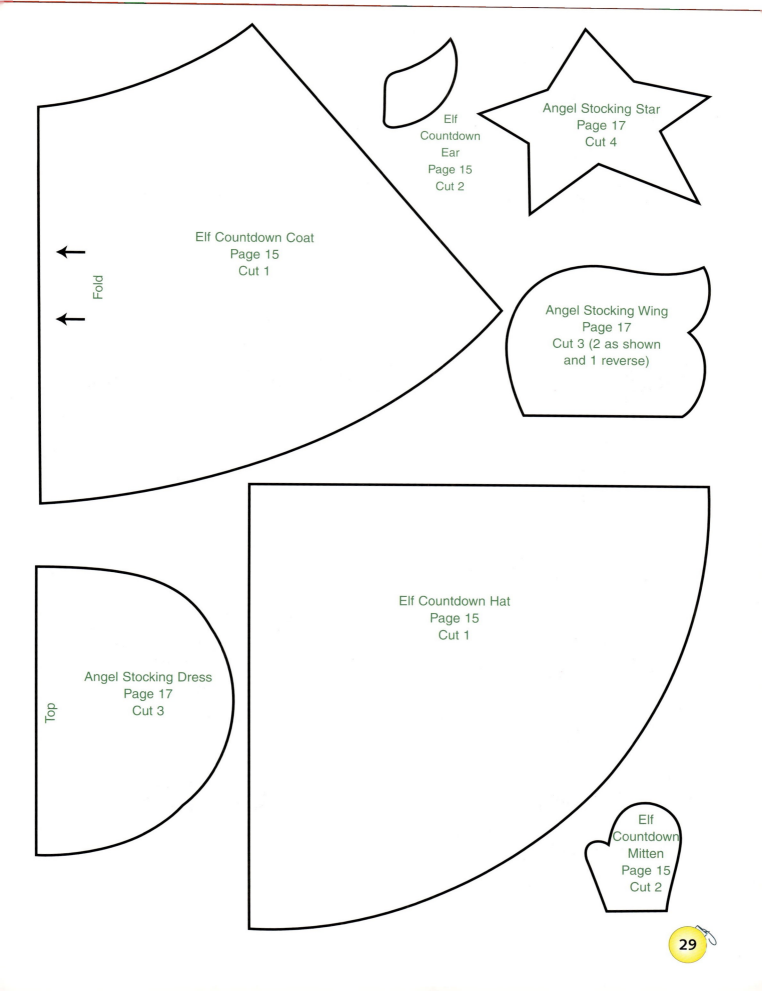

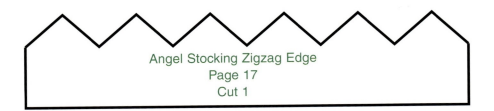

Angel Stocking Zigzag Edge
Page 17
Cut 1

Connect here with tape to make complete stocking

Angel Stocking Bottom
Page 17
Cut 1
Enlarge pattern 200%

Connect here with tape to make complete stocking

Angel Stocking Top
Page 17
Cut 1
Enlarge pattern 200%

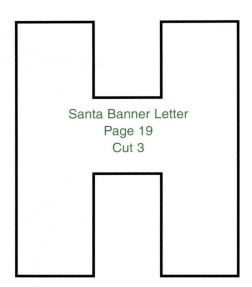

Santa Banner Letter
Page 19
Cut 3

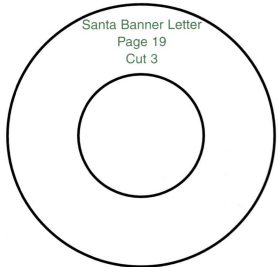

Santa Banner Letter
Page 19
Cut 3

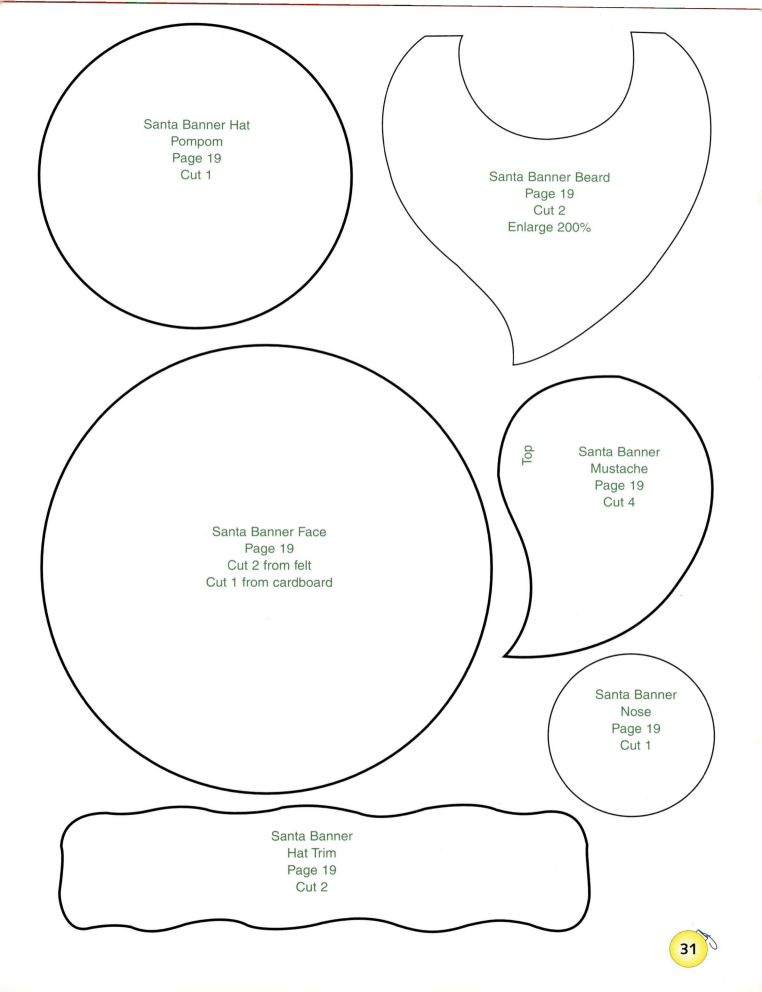

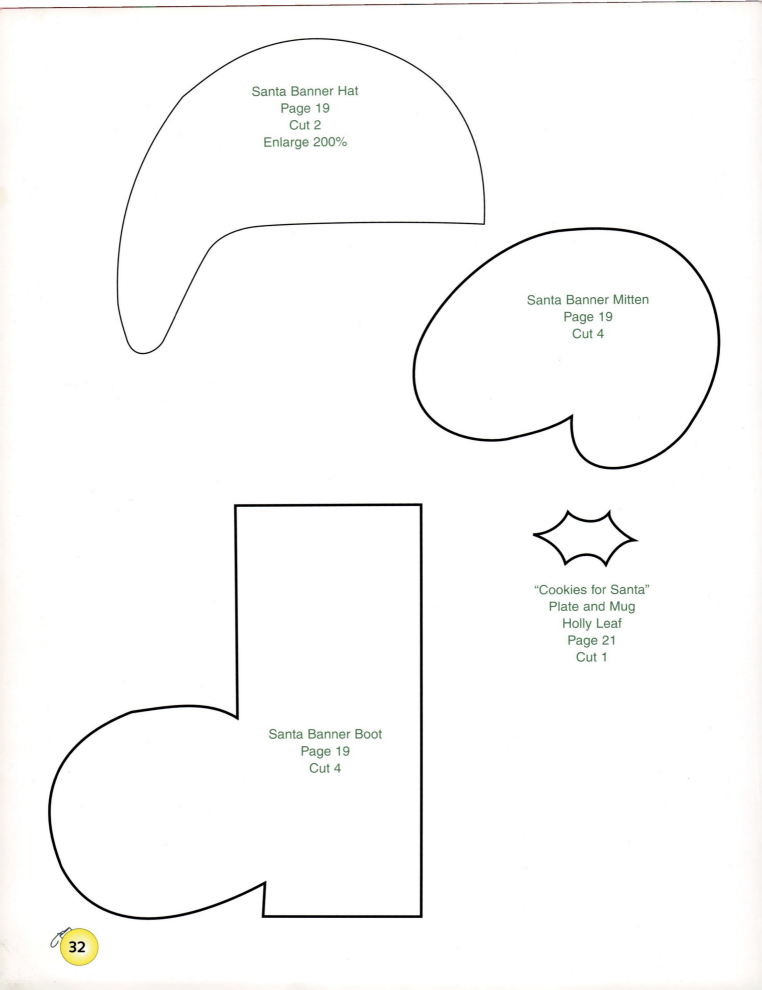